CONTENTS

Not Just an Actor

Chadwick Boseman is best known as an actor. He **portrayed** many people's heroes. Baseball player Jackie Robinson and the superhero Black Panther are two of his big roles, or parts. Boseman also wrote plays and directed movies. Sadly, Boseman passed away in 2020.

AFRICAN AMERICAN SUPERSTARS

CHADWICK BOSEMAN

THERESE M. SHEA

PowerKiDS press.

New York

Published in 2022 by The Rosen Publishing Group, Inc.
29 East 21st Street, New York, NY 10010

First Edition

Editor: Greg Roza
Designer: Rachel Rising

Photo Credits: Cover, pp.1, 19 Emma McIntyre/Staff/Getty Images Entrainment/Getty Images; p. 5 David Crotty/Contributor/Patrick McMullan/Getty Images; p. 7 Paul Bruinooge/Contributor/Patrick McMullan/Getty Images; p. 9 NurPhoto/Contributor/Getty Images; p. 11 The Washington Post/Contributor/Getty Images; p. 13 Kevin Winter/Staff/Getty Images Entrainment/Getty Images; p. 15 D Dipasupil/Contributor/FilmMagic/Getty images; p. 17 Leon Bennett/Contributor/Getty Images Entrainment/Getty Images; p. 20 Charley Gallay/Stringer/Getty Images Entrainment/Getty Images.

Library of Congress Cataloging-in-Publication Data

Names: Shea, Therese, author.
Title: Chadwick Boseman / Therese M. Shea.
Description: New York : PowerKids Press, [2022] | Series: African American superstars | Includes index.
Identifiers: LCCN 2020038454 | ISBN 9781725326033 (library binding) | ISBN 9781725326019 (paperback) | ISBN 9781725326026 (6 pack)
Subjects: LCSH: Boseman, Chadwick–Juvenile literature. | African American actors–Biography–Juvenile literature.
Classification: LCC PN2287.B645 S54 2022 | DDC 791.4302/8092 [B]–dc23
LC record available at https://lccn.loc.gov/2020038454

Manufactured in the United States of America

CPSIA Compliance Information: Batch #CSPK22. For Further Information contact Rosen Publishing, New York, New York at 1-800-237-9932.

BLACK
PANTHER
MARVEL STUDIOS

Early Life

Chadwick Boseman was born November 29, 1976, in Anderson, South Carolina. He has two older brothers. His brother Kevin became a dancer. Kevin had to work hard to make his dream come true. He **inspired** Chadwick to follow his dreams.

High School

In high school, Boseman was a great basketball player. One day, his teammate was shot and killed. To deal with his feelings, Boseman wrote a play. He decided to go to Howard University in Washington, D.C. He wanted to be a director.

HOWARD · UNIVERSITY · WASHINGTON, D.C.
· ET ·
VERITAS
UTILITAS
DEO ET
REIPUB LICÆ

Getting Started

Boseman studied at the British American Drama Academy in England too. After **graduation**, he moved to New York City. He taught acting. He also played roles on a few TV shows, such as *Law & Order* and *Lincoln Heights*.

42

Chadwick Boseman got his big break in the 2013 movie *42*. He played Jackie Robinson. Robinson was the first African American to play Major League Baseball in the 1900s. He faced a lot of **racism** with great bravery.

42
THE TRUE STORY OF AN
AMERICAN LEGEND
RIL 12TH

Get on Up

Boseman's next starring role was *Get on Up* in 2014. This was a movie about famous singer, dancer, and songwriter James Brown. Boseman had to learn to dance like Brown, who was called the "hardest-working man in show business."

FROM THE DIRECTOR OF
THE HELP
CHADWICK
BOSEMAN
NELSAN
ELLIS
ACADEMY AWARD® NOMINEE
VIOLA
DAVIS
ACADEMY AWARD® WINNER
OCTAVIA
SPENCER
GET ON UP
THE JAMES BROWN STOR
AUGUST 1

Marshall

In 2017, Boseman played another hero, Thurgood Marshall, in the movie *Marshall*. Marshall was a lawyer who worked hard to win **civil rights** for all Black Americans. He was later the first African American to become a **Supreme Court justice**.

Black Panther

In 2018, Boseman starred in *Black Panther*. He played T'Challa, the king of a made-up country called Wakanda. T'Challa was also the superhero Black Panther. This was the first comic book movie with a mostly Black cast. It was a huge hit!

MARVEL

Gone Too Soon

On August 28, 2020, Boseman died of cancer. The world was in shock. He had hid his illness from most people even as he helped make more films. His fans were deeply saddened, but they continue to **celebrate** the life and career of Chadwick Boseman.

TIMELINE

November 29, 1976 — Chadwick Boseman is born in Anderson, South Carolina.

2008 — Boseman gets his first continuing role on the TV show *Lincoln Heights.*

2008 — He appears in his first movie, *The Express.*

2013 — Boseman stars as Jackie Robinson in *42*.

2014 — He stars as James Brown in *Get on Up.*

2017 — He portrays Thurgood Marshall in *Marshall*.

2018 — Boseman stars in *Black Panther*.

August 28, 2020 — Boseman passes away from cancer.

GLOSSARY

celebrate: To do something special or enjoyable for an important event or for a important person.

civil rights: The personal freedoms granted to U.S. citizens by law.

graduation: The act of finishing high school or college.

inspire: To move someone to do something.

portray: To play a role.

racism: The belief that one group or race of people is better than another group or race.

Supreme Court justice: A judge on the highest court of the United States.

FOR MORE INFORMATION

BOOKS

Santos, Rita. *Chadwick Boseman: Superstar of Black Panther*. New York, NY: Enslow Publishing, 2019.

Zalewski, Aubrey. *Chadwick Boseman*. North Mankato, MN: Capstone Press, 2019.

WEBSITES

Chadwick Boseman Biography
www.biography.com/actor/chadwick-boseman
Learn much more about the life and career of Chadwick Boseman.

T'Challa/Black Panther
www.marvel.com/characters/black-panther-t-challa
Read more about T'Challa and Black Panther and see clips from the movie *Black Panther*.

Publisher's note to parents and teachers: Our editors have reviewed the websites listed here to make sure they're suitable for students. However, websites may change frequently. Please note that students should always be supervised when they access the internet.

INDEX